I AM MEOW tells the story of a black cat that escaped from his owner, traveled cross country in Lancaster County Pennsylvania and adopted a new family. The new family is very curious about Meow's travels but Meow does not speak human and the adopted family does not speak cat.

Follow Meow's adventure as he creates a new home for himself and brings joy and laughter to his new family as he behaves in his cat-a-wacky way!

As you read about Meow's journey, look carefully for Meow's paw print hidden on each page. See how many paw prints you can find! You'll find the magic number hidden on the last page of the story!

Proceeds from the sale of I AM MEOW will benefit the PET PANTRY of Lancaster, PA.

Robert Ruder - Author
Kelly Gallagher - Illustrator

©2023 Robert Ruder

Hello, I'm a black, boy cat. I say my name a lot so my new human friends decided to name me MEOW.

One day I decided to leave home because my dog brother was always annoying me.

I scooted out the front door when the dog, whose name is WOOF, was let out to use the bathroom.

I must admit it was not a good decision. I knew my human owners would worry about me but WOOF was always pestering me. I needed a quiet, peaceful place to live.

My journey to my new home was very frightening but exciting. I had to travel through an Amish farmer's cornfield.

6

I had to cross a busy country road and not get in the way of an Amish buggy.

I had to walk over a Lancaster County covered bridge.

8

I had to walk through a horse farm.

I had to find safe places to stay during the day and to sleep at night.

I drank water from the Conestoga River and found food to eat in farmers' fields.

My journey was scary. I was brave. I am MEOW.

One day I was walking along the bank of the
Conestoga River not far from a horse farm.
A big human man called to me and made some strange noises.
I decided to see what he wanted.

I walked up to the big gray box that he and the lady called their home. I slowly and carefully climbed up some steps to where the humans lived. I was a little scared.

The lady told the man to give me some food. They were kind humans and the man gave me some milk and bread to eat. I never ate bread before but I was very hungry and it tasted good.

The humans put a big box filled with towels on what they call the deck. I was a little scared but I decided to sleep in the box. It was cozy and warm.

After a while, the man gave me some crunchy food just for cats and a place to go to the bathroom. The lady was very nice to me.

One day the humans invited me into their big gray box. They called their box their home. They let me walk around their home.

The humans started trimming my toenails so I would not hurt their furniture. I like my new home.

I like to look out the openings in the big box
and watch the birds that the humans feed.

Sometimes I like to ZOOM around the inside of my new home and make the humans laugh at me for being so silly.

The man keeps asking me two questions. He wants to know why I left my first home and how I found him and the lady. I have the answers to his questions but he does not understand cat talk and I don't talk human talk.

As I think about my journey, I realized that the world is full of good, kind and loving people whose hearts were warm and open.
I know I can return some love to them.
I'll be a very good house guest.
I AM MEOW!